BUILDING YOUR DREAM BUSINESS

A PRACTICAL GUIDE TO STARTING AND SCALING A SMALL BUSINESS

ANDREW IBRAHIM

Copyright © Andrew Ibrahim
All Rights Reserved.

This book has been self-published with all reasonable efforts taken to make the material error-free by the author. No part of this book shall be used, reproduced in any manner whatsoever without written permission from the author, except in the case of brief quotations embodied in critical articles and reviews.

The Author of this book is solely responsible and liable for its content including but not limited to the views, representations, descriptions, statements, information, opinions and references ["Content"]. The Content of this book shall not constitute or be construed or deemed to reflect the opinion or expression of the Publisher or Editor. Neither the Publisher nor Editor endorse or approve the Content of this book or guarantee the reliability, accuracy or completeness of the Content published herein and do not make any representations or warranties of any kind, express or implied, including but not limited to the implied warranties of merchantability, fitness for a particular purpose. The Publisher and Editor shall not be liable whatsoever for any errors, omissions, whether such errors or omissions result from negligence, accident, or any other cause or claims for loss or damages of any kind, including without limitation, indirect or consequential loss or damage arising out of use, inability to use, or about the reliability, accuracy or sufficiency of the information contained in this book.

Made with ♥ on the Notion Press Platform
www.notionpress.com

This book is dedicated to all small business owners and entrepreneurs who have the courage and determination to turn their dreams into reality. May this guidebook be a valuable resource in your journey to success.

Contents

Contents

Foreword

As a seasoned entrepreneur and business consultant, I have had the privilege of working with Andrew Ibrahim and have seen firsthand the passion and dedication he brings to his work. His knowledge and expertise in the field of small business are unparalleled, and I have no doubt that this guidebook will be a valuable resource for any entrepreneur looking to start or grow their business.

In "Building Your Dream Business," Andrew provides a step-by-step guide to starting and running a successful business, covering everything from market research and financial management to marketing strategies and operations. He draws on his own experiences and expertise to provide practical tips and real-world examples that will help readers navigate the complexities of starting and running a business.

I highly recommend this guidebook to anyone who is thinking about starting a small business or who has recently started one and wants to learn more about how to make it successful. Andrew's knowledge and expertise will give you the confidence to make informed decisions and reach your desired financial outcomes. With the right mindset and the right tools, you'll be able to navigate the marketplace, stand out from the competition, and turn your small business into a thriving enterprise that truly connects with its customers.

Preface

As the author of "Building Your Dream Business: A Step-by-Step Guide to Starting and Running a Successful Business," it is my pleasure to introduce this comprehensive guidebook to aspiring entrepreneurs. This book is the culmination of my years of experience and expertise in the industry, and it is my hope that it will provide readers with a clear and actionable roadmap for success.

Throughout the pages of this book, I have included a wealth of information on topics such as market research, financial management, marketing strategies, and operations. Drawing on real-world examples and my own personal experiences, I have provided practical tips and advice that are relevant and easy to understand. Whether you're a new entrepreneur just starting out or an experienced business owner looking to take your business to the next level, this guidebook is for you.

It has been my passion to help small businesses succeed, and this book is a reflection of that passion. I have poured my heart and soul into creating a resource that will be valuable to anyone looking to start or grow their small business. I truly believe that with the right mindset and the right tools, anyone can achieve their business dreams.

I would like to extend my gratitude to all the entrepreneurs and business owners who have shared their stories and experiences with me, as well as the team at OpenAI for their support and guidance in the creation of this book.

As you embark on your journey to starting and running a successful small business, I hope that this book will be a valuable resource for you every step of the way.

Acknowledgements

I would like to extend my deepest gratitude to all of the individuals who have helped me in the creation of this book.

First and foremost, I would like to thank my family and friends for their unwavering support and encouragement throughout this journey. Their love and understanding has been invaluable to me.

I would also like to thank my team of editors and beta readers who have provided invaluable feedback and helped to shape the final product. Their insights and suggestions have been invaluable in making this book as helpful as possible.

I am also grateful for the small business owners who shared their stories and experiences with me. Their willingness to share their successes and challenges has provided valuable insights and inspiration for this book.

Finally, I would like to thank the team at OpenAI for providing the training data, guidance and support that helped me to write this book.

This book would not have been possible without the contributions of each and every one of these individuals. Thank you all for your support and for being a part of this journey.

Prologue

"Building Your Dream Business" is a journey that begins with a spark of an idea, a passion, and a determination to succeed. It is a journey that requires dedication, hard work, and a willingness to take risks. This book is a guide for anyone who has ever dreamed of starting their own business. It is for anyone who wants to turn their passion into a reality and build a successful enterprise that truly connects with its customers.

In this book, I will take you through the journey of starting and running a small business, from the very first steps of market research and financial management to the ongoing challenges of marketing and operations. I will share with you my own experiences and the lessons I've learned, as well as the stories of other entrepreneurs who have successfully built their own businesses.

I will show you how to navigate the complexities of starting a business, and provide you with the tools and strategies you need to turn your dream into a reality. I will also guide you through the challenges you will face along the way, and offer words of encouragement to help you stay motivated and focused on your goals.

This book is for anyone who is thinking about starting a small business, or who has recently started one and wants to learn more about how to make it successful. It is for anyone who is willing to put in the work to make their dream a reality. With the right mindset and the right tools, anyone can turn their small business into a thriving enterprise that truly connects with its customers.

So, let's begin this journey together, let's build your dream business!

CHAPTER ONE

Introduction

As you embark on this journey, it's important to remember that starting a small business can be challenging, but it's also incredibly rewarding. You'll have the opportunity to pursue your passions, create something of your own, and make a difference in the world. With the right mindset and the right tools, anything is possible.

In this guidebook, you'll find actionable advice, real-world examples, and practical tips that will help you to overcome the most common challenges faced by small businesses. You'll also learn about the latest trends and best practices in the industry. But this guidebook is not just about providing you with information, it's also about empowering you to take action.

As you read through the guidebook, you'll learn how to:

- Conduct market research to identify your target market and competition
- Create a budget and financial plan
- Develop a marketing strategy that will help you stand out in a crowded market
- Manage your operations and streamline your processes
- Build a team and hire the right employees
- Scale your business and achieve growth

We're excited to be a part of your small business journey and we can't wait to see what you'll achieve. Remember that success is not a destination, it's a journey. And with this guidebook by your side, you'll be well on your way to building your dream business.

Case Study

Meet John, a recent college graduate who has always had a passion for photography. He wants to start his own photography business, but he's not sure where to begin. Like many new entrepreneurs, John doesn't know how to conduct market research, manage his finances, or create a marketing plan.

That's where our guidebook comes in. By reading the Market Research section, John learns how to identify his target market and conduct a SWOT analysis to identify the strengths, weaknesses, opportunities, and threats of his business. He also identifies his competition and learns how to set himself apart.

With the help of the Financial Management section, John sets financial goals, creates a budget, and learns how to manage cash flow and understand financial statements. He also learns how to raise capital to invest in his business.

By reading the Marketing Strategies section, John develops a marketing plan that targets his target audience and chooses the right marketing channels, such as social media, to reach them. He also learns how to measure the success of his marketing efforts and adapt to changing market conditions.

Thanks to the advice and guidance provided in our guidebook, John is able to turn his passion for photography into a successful business. Today, he's a sought-after wedding photographer, with a growing list of satisfied customers and a business that generates a healthy profit.

CHAPTER THREE

Market Research

The Market Research section of our guidebook is designed to help you understand your target market and competition, as well as conduct a SWOT analysis to identify your strengths, weaknesses, opportunities, and threats of your business.

The section will cover the following topics:

- Understanding your target market: This section will provide guidance on how to identify and segment your target market, including demographics, psychographics, and buying habits.
- Identifying your competition: This section will help you understand your competition and how to position yourself in the market. This includes analyzing the competition's strengths, weaknesses, and target market.
- Conducting a SWOT analysis: This section will guide you on how to conduct a SWOT analysis to identify your strengths, weaknesses, opportunities and threats of your business. This will allow you to make better-informed decisions about the direction of your business.

By the end of this section, you will have a clear understanding of your target market and competition, as well as an analysis of your own business's strengths and weaknesses. This information will be crucial as you move on to develop your financial and marketing plans.

Understanding your Target Market

Understanding your Target Market is a crucial step in starting and running a successful small business. It helps you identify the specific group of people you want to reach with your products or services and tailor your marketing strategies to meet their needs. The section will provide guidance on how to identify and segment your target market by understanding their demographics, psychographics and buying habits.

For example, let's say you are starting a clothing line for kids. By identifying the demographics of your target market such as age range, gender and income level, you can tailor your clothing designs and prices accordingly. You may find that the majority of your target market is made up of parents with children aged between 3-8 years old and have an average income of $50,000 per year. With this information, you can design clothes that appeal to children in that age range and price them accordingly for your target market's income level.

Psychographics can also play a crucial role in understanding your target market. For example, if you found out that your target market values eco-friendly and sustainable products, you can make sure that your clothing line uses environmentally friendly materials and production methods, which will help you to attract and retain customers who share those values.

By analyzing buying habits, you can understand the best way to reach and persuade your target market to buy your products or services. For example, if you found out that your target market primarily shops online, you can make sure that your online store is easy to navigate and provides a seamless shopping experience.

Overall, by understanding your target market, you can make better-informed decisions about your business, including product development, marketing strategies, and overall business direction. This can help you to attract and retain customers, increase sales and achieve long-term success.

Identifying your Competition

Identifying your Competition is an important step in starting and running a successful small business. It helps entrepreneurs understand the other players in the market and how to position themselves in relation to them. The section will provide guidance on how to analyze the competition's strengths, weaknesses, and target market.

For example, let's say you're starting a coffee shop in a busy downtown area. By identifying your competition, you can see what other coffee shops are in the area and what they offer. You may find that the competition primarily serves premium, artisanal coffee and has a trendy, minimalist decor. With this information, you can position yourself as a more budget-friendly option while still offering high-quality coffee, or you can differentiate yourself by offering a wider variety of flavors and brewing methods.

By analyzing the competition's strengths and weaknesses, you can understand their business model and the areas in which they excel and the areas they lack in. For example, if you found out that your competition's main strength is their fast service, you can focus on providing a comfortable and relaxing atmosphere for your customers.

By understanding your competition's target market, you can see who they are trying to reach and how you can appeal to a slightly different group of customers. For example, you may find that your competition targets young professionals, and you can focus on targeting families or students.

Overall, by identifying your competition, you can make better-informed decisions about your business, including product development, marketing strategies, and overall business direction. This can help you to attract and retain customers, increase sales and achieve long-term success.

Conducting a SWOT Analysis

Conducting a SWOT Analysis is an incredibly valuable tool for entrepreneurs. It's like having a crystal ball that helps you see the future of your business. By taking the time to analyze your business's Strengths, Weaknesses, Opportunities, and Threats, you'll be able to make better-informed decisions about the direction of your business.

Let's say, for example, you're starting a new software development company. By conducting a SWOT analysis, you'll be able to see what you're doing right and where you might need to improve. For example, you might find that your team of experienced developers is a huge strength, but that you lack marketing experience. Or, you might see that there's a growing demand for software development services in your area, which could be a huge opportunity for your business. At the same time, you might also see that there's fierce competition in the market, which could be a threat to your business.

Once you've identified these areas, you can make better-informed decisions about the direction of your business. For example, you might decide to invest in marketing strategies to promote your company and hire a marketing specialist to help you stand out from the competition. Or, you might decide to focus on building a competitive advantage by leveraging your team of experienced developers.

Overall, by conducting a SWOT analysis, you'll be able to make better-informed decisions about your business, including product development, marketing strategies, and overall business direction. This can help you to attract and retain customers, increase sales, and achieve long-term success. It's like having a roadmap for your business, and it's an essential tool for any entrepreneur who wants to achieve success.

CHAPTER FOUR

Financial Management

Financial Management is a vital component of starting and running a successful small business. It's like having a GPS for your business finances, guiding you on the path to success. This section of the guidebook will provide step-by-step guidance on how to effectively manage cash flow, set financial goals, create a budget, and understand financial statements.

For example, let's say you're starting a new bakery. As a business owner, you'll need to make sure you have enough money on hand to pay your bills and purchase ingredients, even during slower sales periods. By effectively managing your cash flow, you'll be able to stay afloat during these times and make sure your bakery never runs out of supplies.

Setting financial goals is another important aspect of financial management. It's like having a roadmap for your business, it helps you measure your progress and make adjustments as needed. For example, you might set a goal to double your sales within the next year, this will give you a clear target to work towards and help you track your progress.

Creating a budget is also an important part of financial management, it helps you keep your expenses under control and make sure you're on track to achieve your financial goals. For example, if you notice that your expenses are higher than your income, you'll know that you need to cut costs or increase sales.

Understanding your financial statements is also important. it's like reading the story of your business, it can help you see how your business is performing and identify areas where you might need to make changes. For example, if you notice that your expenses are higher than your income, you'll know that you need to cut costs or increase sales.

Overall, by practicing good financial management, you'll be able to keep your business on a strong financial footing and achieve long-term success. It's like having a personal financial advisor for your business, which can give you the confidence to make informed decisions and grow your business. With the right financial management strategies in place, you'll be able to turn your small business into a thriving enterprise.

Setting financial goals

Setting financial goals is a crucial step in managing the financial aspect of a small business. It's like having a roadmap for your business finances, helping you measure your progress, and make adjustments as needed. This section will provide guidance on how to set realistic, measurable, and achievable financial goals for your business.

For example, let's say you're starting a new retail store. By setting financial goals, you'll be able to measure your progress and make adjustments as needed. For example, you might set a goal to increase your sales by 20% within the next year. This will give you a clear target to work towards and help you track your progress. By regularly reviewing your financials, you'll be able to measure how close you are to reaching your goal and make adjustments as needed.

But setting financial goals isn't just about looking at numbers, it's also about understanding your target market, identifying areas of growth, and creating a plan of action. For example, if you notice that your sales are not growing as fast as you had hoped, you might need to invest more in understanding your target market and identifying new areas of growth. This might mean researching your competitors, identifying new trends in your industry, or focusing on a specific market segment.

By setting financial goals and working towards them, you'll be able to make informed decisions about where to invest your resources and how to grow your business. It's like having a personal financial coach for your business, which can give you the confidence to make informed decisions and reach your desired financial outcomes. Setting financial goals will help you focus on what's important, prioritize your efforts, and make sure your business is moving in the right direction. With the right financial goals in place, you'll be able to turn your small business into a thriving enterprise.

Creating a budget

Creating a budget is a crucial step in managing the financial aspect of a small business, it's like having a map for your business finances, guiding you on the path to success. This section of the guidebook will provide step-by-step guidance on how to effectively create a budget that works for your business.

For example, let's say you're starting a new consulting business. It's important to have a clear picture of where your money is going and make sure you're not overspending in any areas. This might mean setting a budget for things like office expenses, marketing, employee salaries, and other operational expenses. By regularly reviewing your budget, comparing it to your actual expenses, and making adjustments as needed, you'll be able to identify areas where you might need to make changes and optimize your budget for maximum efficiency.

Creating a budget is not just about numbers, it's also about understanding your business, identifying areas of growth, and creating a plan of action. For example, if you notice that your marketing expenses are higher than you had planned, you might need to focus on developing more cost-effective marketing strategies, identifying new areas of growth, or exploring new revenue streams to increase your income.

Overall, by creating a budget, you'll be able to keep your expenses under control and make sure you're on track to achieve your financial goals. It's like having a personal financial advisor for your business, which can give you the confidence to make informed decisions and reach your desired financial outcomes. Setting a budget will help you focus on what's important, prioritize your efforts, and make sure your business is moving in the right direction. With the right budget in place, you'll be able to turn your small business into a thriving enterprise.

Managing cash flow

Managing cash flow is a critical aspect of running a successful small business. It's like having a pulse on the financial health of your business, helping you ensure that you have enough money on hand to pay bills and invest in growth opportunities. This section of the guidebook will provide guidance on how to effectively manage cash flow to keep your business financially stable.

For example, let's say you're starting a new landscaping business. Managing cash flow is crucial to ensure you have enough money on hand to pay bills and purchase materials, even during slower periods of business. By creating a cash flow projection, you'll be able to forecast when you'll have more or less money coming in, and adjust your spending accordingly. This might mean holding off on hiring new employees or postponing a large equipment purchase during a slow period, but investing in a new marketing campaign during a busy season.

Managing cash flow is not just about numbers, it's also about understanding your business cycle and identifying opportunities for growth. For example, if you notice that you have a large influx of cash during a certain period, you might want to consider investing in new equipment, hiring new employees, or expanding to a new location.

Overall, by effectively managing cash flow, you'll be able to keep your business financially stable and take advantage of growth opportunities when they arise. It's like having a personal financial advisor for your business, which can give you the confidence to make informed decisions and reach your desired financial outcomes. Managing cash flow will help you focus on what's important, prioritize your efforts, and make sure your business is moving in the right direction. With a solid cash flow management plan in place, you'll be able to turn your small business into a thriving enterprise.

Understanding financial statements

Understanding financial statements is a key aspect of managing the financial side of a small business. It's like having a window into the inner workings of your business, helping you see how your business is performing and identify areas where you might need to make changes. This section of the guidebook will provide guidance on how to read and understand financial statements, including income statements, balance sheets, and cash flow statements.

For example, let's say you're starting a new online store. Understanding your financial statements is crucial to see how your business is performing and identify areas where you might need to make changes. By regularly reviewing your income statement, you'll be able to see how much revenue your business is generating, and compare it to your expenses to see if you're making a profit or a loss. By reviewing your balance sheet, you'll be able to see how much assets and liabilities your business has, and assess your business's overall financial health. And by reviewing your cash flow statement, you'll be able to see how much cash is flowing in and out of your business, and make sure you have enough cash on hand to pay bills and invest in growth opportunities.

Understanding financial statements is not just about numbers, it's also about understanding your business and identifying areas of growth. For example, if you notice that your expenses are higher than your income, you might need to cut costs or increase sales. Or if you notice that your assets are not growing as fast as you had hoped, you might need to invest more in building your business.

Overall, by understanding your financial statements, you'll be able to see how your business is performing and identify areas where you might need to make changes. It's like having a personal financial advisor for your business, which can give you the confidence to make informed decisions and reach your desired financial outcomes. Understanding financial statements will help you focus on what's important, prioritize your efforts, and make sure your business is moving in the right direction. With a solid understanding of your financial statements, you'll be able to make better-informed decisions about product development, marketing strategies, and overall business direction. This can help you attract and retain customers, increase sales, and achieve long-term success.

Raising capital

Raising capital is a critical component of starting and growing a small business. Think of it as the gasoline that propels your business forward, providing the necessary resources to invest in growth and expansion opportunities. This section of the guidebook will provide valuable guidance on how to raise capital for your small business, including through loans, grants, and investment opportunities.

For instance, imagine you're launching a new e-commerce platform. To bring your vision to life, you'll need to raise capital to fund product development, assemble a team, and get your business up and running. One way to secure funding is by applying for a small business loan from a bank or government agency. Another option is to seek out grants from organizations that support small businesses. And for more seasoned entrepreneurs, you could also raise capital through angel investors or venture capitalists, who can provide not only funding but also invaluable mentorship and connections.

Raising capital is not just about acquiring funding, it's also about understanding your business and identifying opportunities for growth. For example, if you realize that you need to hire more staff or invest in new technology, you may need to explore different ways of raising capital.

In summary, by raising capital, you'll be able to invest in growth and expansion opportunities, which can help you take your business to the next level. It's like having a personal financial advisor for your business, which can give you the confidence to make informed decisions and reach your desired financial outcomes. Raising capital will help you focus on what's important, prioritize your efforts, and make sure your business is moving in the right direction. With the right funding in place, you'll be able to turn your small business into a thriving enterprise.

Marketing Strategies

Marketing Strategies is a key aspect of starting and growing a small business. It's like having a compass for your business, helping you navigate the marketplace and reach your target customers. This section of the guidebook will provide guidance on how to develop effective marketing strategies for your small business, including online and offline methods, branding, and customer engagement.

For example, let's say you're starting a new landscaping business. By developing effective marketing strategies, you'll be able to reach your target customers and grow your business. This might mean creating a website, running social media campaigns, and building relationships with local real estate agents and other referral sources. By understanding your target market and their needs, you'll be able to create a messaging and branding that resonates with them and stands out in the market.

Marketing strategies also help you to stay on top of the competition, identify new opportunities, and make sure you have a solid plan to generate leads and convert them into paying customers. For example, if you notice that your competitors are using a particular marketing technique that seems to be working well, you might want to consider incorporating that technique into your own marketing strategy.

Overall, by developing effective marketing strategies, you'll be able to reach your target customers, grow your business, and achieve long-term success. It's like having a personal marketing advisor for your business, which can give you the confidence to make informed decisions and reach your desired financial outcomes. With a solid marketing strategy in place, you'll be able to navigate the marketplace, stand out from the competition, and turn your small business into a thriving enterprise.

Creating a winning marketing plan

Creating a winning marketing plan is the key to making your small business soar! It's like having a map to guide you on your journey to success, helping you navigate the competitive marketplace and connect with your target customers. This section of the guidebook will provide you with all the tools you need to develop a comprehensive marketing plan that will take your business to the next level. You will learn how to conduct market research, identify your unique selling proposition, and set goals that are specific, measurable and achievable.

Imagine you're starting a new tutoring business, and you want to reach out to parents of school-aged children. By developing a marketing plan, you'll be able to identify the needs and preferences of your target market and tailor your services to meet them. You'll also be able to highlight your unique selling proposition, perhaps emphasizing your experience as a teacher, to set your business apart from the competition. And with specific, measurable and achievable marketing goals, such as increasing your client base by 20% within the next year, you'll have a clear roadmap to follow and a way to track your progress.

But a marketing plan isn't just about creating a plan and forgetting it, it's also about staying agile and making adjustments as needed. For example, if you notice that your marketing efforts are not producing the desired results, you can make changes to your plan and try different approaches.

By developing a comprehensive marketing plan, you'll be able to reach your target customers, grow your business, and achieve long-term success. It's like having a personal marketing advisor for your business, which can give you the confidence to make informed decisions and reach your desired financial outcomes. With a solid marketing plan in place, you'll be able to navigate the marketplace, stand out from the competition, and turn your small business into a thriving enterprise that you can be proud of. So, get ready to take your business to the next level, and let's create that winning marketing plan together!

Choosing the right marketing channels

Choosing the right marketing channels is a game-changer for small businesses. Imagine having a secret weapon that helps you reach your target audience exactly where they're hanging out and speaking their language. This section of the guidebook is going to unlock that secret weapon for you, by providing expert guidance on how to select the most effective marketing channels for your small business. Whether it's traditional methods such as print ads and direct mail, or digital channels like social media and email marketing, you'll learn how to make strategic decisions that will help you connect with your target audience in a meaningful way.

Take for example, a new restaurant owner looking to attract more customers. By choosing the right marketing channels, you could reach your target audience where they are spending their time like on food review websites, food blogs and social media platforms like Instagram and Facebook. By sharing mouth-watering images of your food, running promotions and engaging with your target audience, you'll be able to attract new customers and keep them coming back for more.

But the best part is, that choosing the right marketing channels isn't just about selecting the most popular options, it's also about understanding the unique needs and preferences of your target audience. By truly understanding your customers, you'll be able to select the channels that will resonate with them and create a marketing plan that truly connects with them on a deeper level.

Overall, by choosing the right marketing channels, you'll be able to reach your target audience where they are and create a marketing plan that resonates with them. It's like having a secret weapon that helps you stand out from the competition and turn your small business into a thriving enterprise that truly connects with its customers. Are you ready to take your marketing game to the next level? Let's do this!

Measuring marketing success

Measuring marketing success is like having a crystal ball for your business, giving you valuable insights into how your marketing efforts are impacting your bottom line. By understanding what's working and what's not, you can make strategic adjustments and optimize your marketing strategies for maximum impact. In this section of the guidebook, you'll learn how to set measurable goals, track key metrics, and analyze data to gain a deeper understanding of your customers and their needs.

For example, let's say you're starting a new landscaping business and you want to increase your online presence. By setting measurable goals, such as increasing your website traffic by 30% within the next 3 months, you'll be able to track your progress and make adjustments as needed. By tracking metrics such as search engine rankings, social media engagement, and customer feedback, you'll be able to understand how your marketing efforts are impacting your business. And by analyzing data, you'll be able to identify patterns and insights that can inform your future marketing strategies.

Measuring marketing success is not just about numbers, it's also about understanding your customers and their needs. For example, if you notice that your social media engagement is high but your website traffic is low, you might need to focus on optimizing your website for better user experience.

Overall, by measuring marketing success, you'll be able to make data-driven decisions and fine-tune your marketing strategies for maximum impact. It's like having a personal marketing advisor for your business, giving you the confidence to make informed decisions and reach your desired financial outcomes. By understanding what's working and what's not, you'll be able to navigate the marketplace, stand out from the competition, and turn your small business into a thriving enterprise that truly connects with its customers and understands their needs. It's an exciting journey that will help you to grow your business and achieve your goals.

Adapting to changing market conditions

Adapting to changing market conditions is a crucial step in creating sustainable marketing strategies for a small business. It's like having a crystal ball for your business, helping you anticipate the future and make adjustments to your marketing plan before it's too late. This section of the guidebook will provide guidance on how to stay ahead of market trends, anticipate shifts in consumer behavior, and make adjustments to your marketing plan as needed.

For example, imagine you're running a new age bookstore and you want to stay ahead of the latest trends in spirituality and wellness. By keeping an eye on market conditions, you'll be able to anticipate shifts in consumer behavior, such as an increased demand for mindfulness and meditation practices. By adapting your marketing strategies to reflect these trends, you'll be able to attract new customers and stay relevant in the market.

Adapting to changing market conditions is not just about following the latest trends, it's also about understanding your customers and their needs. For example, if you notice that your target audience is increasingly interested in online workshops and webinars, you might need to invest in online tools and resources to support this.

Overall, by adapting to changing market conditions, you'll be able to stay ahead of the competition and create sustainable marketing strategies that resonate with your target audience. It's like having a personal marketing advisor for your business, which can give you the confidence to make informed decisions and reach your desired financial outcomes. With the ability to adapt to changing market conditions, you'll be able to navigate the marketplace, stay relevant and turn your small business into a thriving enterprise that truly connects with its customers and adapts to their ever-changing needs.

CHAPTER SIX

Operations

Operations is the backbone of any small business. It's the unsung hero that keeps everything running like a well-oiled machine. This section of the guidebook will provide guidance on how to streamline your business operations, increase efficiency, and improve overall performance. And let me tell you, there's nothing more exciting than a smooth-running business!

Imagine you're starting a new e-commerce business. By streamlining your operations, you'll be able to manage your inventory and supplies like a pro, ensuring that you have the right products in stock at all times. By automating certain processes, such as order fulfillment and shipping, you'll be able to improve production and logistics, resulting in lightning-fast delivery times and customers who are happier than a kid in a candy store.

But streamlining operations is not just about technology, it's also about understanding your customers and their needs. For example, if you notice that your customers value fast delivery times, you might need to invest in better logistics and shipping options to meet that need. And that's the beauty of streamlining operations - it's all about finding ways to make your business run more smoothly and efficiently, while also meeting the needs of your customers.

Overall, by streamlining operations, you'll be able to improve efficiency and performance, which can help you take your business to the next level. It's like having a personal operations advisor for your business, which can give you the confidence to make informed decisions and reach your desired financial outcomes. With streamlined operations, you'll be able to navigate the marketplace, stand out from the competition, and turn your small business into a thriving enterprise that truly understands and meets the needs of its customers. So, get ready to streamline your operations, and watch as your business transforms into a well-oiled machine!

Setting up shop

Setting up shop is a vital step in launching and running a successful small business. It's like building the foundation for your business, providing the necessary infrastructure to support your operations and connect with your customers. This section of the guidebook will show you how to establish a physical or online storefront that's tailored to your brand and values, choose the ideal location, and create a space that resonates with your target audience.

Imagine you're opening a new coffee shop. By setting up shop, you'll be able to pick the perfect spot, such as a bustling downtown area with high foot traffic, to attract customers. Additionally, you'll be able to design a space that aligns with your brand and values, such as a cozy, inviting atmosphere with the aroma of fresh coffee beans filling the air.

However, setting up shop is not just about the physical space, it's also about understanding your customers and their needs. For instance, if you notice that many of your customers are looking for a quick and convenient option, you might need to invest in online ordering and delivery options to meet that need.

In conclusion, by setting up shop, you'll be able to create a space that aligns with your brand and values and appeals to your target audience. It's like having a personal design advisor for your business, which can give you the confidence to make informed decisions and reach your desired financial outcomes. With the right setup in place, you'll be able to navigate the marketplace, stand out from the competition, and turn your small business into a thriving enterprise that truly connects with its customers.

Choosing the right location

When it comes to opening a small business, choosing the right location is crucial. It's like finding the perfect real estate for your business to thrive. This guidebook will show you how to find the ideal spot to set up shop, taking into account the local market, high-traffic areas, and the needs of your target audience.

Imagine you're opening a new coffee shop. You want to make sure you're in a place that's easily accessible for your customers, and where they'll be able to find you easily. By assessing the local market, you may find that a busy downtown area with lots of foot traffic is the perfect spot for your coffee shop, ensuring that your business is visible and easily accessible for your customers.

Choosing the right location is not just about finding the right spot, it's also about understanding the needs and preferences of your target audience. For example, if your target audience is primarily younger adults, you may want to focus on setting up shop in an area with a vibrant nightlife or near a college campus.

By choosing the ideal location, you'll be able to attract more customers, increase visibility and put your business on the path to success. It's like having a personal location advisor for your business, giving you the confidence to make informed decisions and reach your desired financial outcomes. With the perfect location, you'll be able to navigate the marketplace, stand out from the competition, and turn your small business into a thriving enterprise that truly connects with its customers.

Managing inventory

Managing inventory is a vital aspect of running a small business. It's like being the conductor of an orchestra, making sure all the right pieces are in place and ready to play at the right time. This section of the guidebook will provide guidance on how to effectively manage your inventory, including forecasting demand, implementing an inventory management system, and monitoring stock levels.

For example, let's say you're running a clothing boutique. By managing your inventory effectively, you'll be able to predict which styles and sizes will be most popular, ensuring that you always have the right items in stock to meet customer demand. By implementing an inventory management system, such as barcode scanning or automated inventory software, you'll be able to easily track stock levels and reorder items as needed.

But managing inventory is not just about numbers, it's also about understanding your customers and their needs. For example, if you notice that your customers are increasingly interested in sustainable and ethically-produced clothing, you might need to adjust your inventory to reflect that.

Overall, by managing inventory effectively, you'll be able to improve efficiency, increase customer satisfaction, and take your business to the next level. It's like having a personal inventory advisor for your business, which can give you the confidence to make informed decisions and reach your desired financial outcomes. With effective inventory management, you'll be able to navigate the marketplace, stand out from the competition, and turn your small business into a thriving enterprise that truly understands and meets the needs of its customers.

Hiring and managing employees

Hiring and managing employees is a vital component of any small business, as having the right team can take your business to new heights of success! Imagine assembling a dream team of individuals who possess not only the necessary skills but also a passion for helping your business thrive. This section of the guidebook will provide you with the tools you need to hire the best employees, create a work environment that fosters growth and positivity, and effectively manage and motivate your team to perform at their absolute best.

Take for instance, you've just opened a new restaurant and you're looking to hire a team of servers who are not only knowledgeable about food and wine but also possess great customer service skills. By creating a positive work culture, providing regular training and incentives, and valuing employee feedback, you'll be able to attract and retain top talent.

But hiring and managing employees is not just about assembling the right team, it's also about understanding the unique needs and preferences of each individual. For example, if you notice that your employees are struggling with work-life balance, you might need to consider offering flexible scheduling options to meet that need.

Overall, by hiring and managing employees effectively, you'll be able to take your small business to the next level! You'll have a team of individuals who are passionate about the success of your business, and who will work hard to achieve your goals. It's like having a personal human resources advisor for your business, which can give you the confidence to make informed decisions and reach your desired financial outcomes. With the right team in place, you'll be able to navigate the marketplace, stand out from the competition, and turn your small business into a thriving enterprise that truly connects with its customers and employees.

Legal and Lincenesing

When it comes to running a small business, "legal and compliance issues" can feel like a heavy burden. But the truth is, navigating these issues is crucial for the long-term success of your business. Think of it like having a shield that protects your business from potential legal problems and compliance violations.

In this section of the guidebook, we'll show you how to navigate the legal and compliance landscape with ease. We'll help you understand relevant laws and regulations, and provide guidance on how to develop policies and procedures to ensure compliance.

For example, imagine you're starting a new technology company. By understanding legal and compliance issues, you'll be able to protect your business from potential legal issues related to data privacy and intellectual property. You'll be able to develop policies and procedures that ensure compliance with industry standards and regulations.

But it's not all about protecting your business, it's also about understanding the needs and preferences of your customers and employees. For example, if you notice that your employees are struggling with understanding their rights and responsibilities, you might need to provide training and resources to meet that need.

By understanding and addressing legal and compliance issues, you'll be able to protect your business, and ensure its long-term success. It's like having a personal legal advisor for your business, giving you the confidence to make informed decisions and reach your desired financial outcomes. With a solid understanding of legal and compliance issues, you'll be able to navigate the marketplace, stand out from the competition, and turn your small business into a thriving enterprise that is compliant and protected. So let's dive in and take control of your legal and compliance issues with confidence and excitement!

Conclusion

Congratulations! You've made it to the end of this guidebook for starting and running a successful small business. By reaching the conclusion, you've accomplished a huge feat - you've taken the first steps to turn your dream into a reality. By following the guidance provided in this guidebook, you've learned how to conduct market research, create a budget, develop a marketing plan, and navigate the many complexities of starting and running a small business. You've come a long way and should be proud of your progress.

But the journey doesn't stop here. Now, it's time to reflect on all that you've accomplished, celebrate your successes, and identify areas for improvement. By reviewing your progress, you'll be able to pinpoint the strategies that have worked well and the ones that need a little tweaking. By planning for the future, you'll be able to set new goals and take your business to the next level. The possibilities are endless and the sky's the limit.

But remember, the marketplace is ever-changing and new trends are always emerging. It's important to always be prepared for what's to come and be willing to adapt. By staying informed and having an open mind, you'll be able to navigate the marketplace and stay relevant.

So, don't stop now! Keep pushing forward, stay determined and believe in yourself. With the right mindset and the right tools, you'll be able to turn your small business into a thriving enterprise that truly connects with its customers. The best is yet to come!

Final thoughts and encouragement

Final thoughts and encouragement is the crowning moment of your small business journey. It's like reaching the summit of a mountain, where you can look back on the path you've taken and feel a sense of accomplishment and pride. This section of the guidebook will provide guidance on how to reflect on your journey, celebrate your successes, and stay motivated and energized to continue on your path to success.

For example, imagine you've been using our guidebook to help you navigate the complexities of starting and running a business. You've made it through the ups and downs and have arrived at the final thoughts and encouragement section. Now is the time to take a step back and reflect on everything you've learned and accomplished. You'll be able to identify what worked well for you and what didn't, and take away valuable insights that you can apply to your future business ventures. And with the encouragement provided in this section, you'll be able to stay motivated and energized to tackle any challenges that come your way.

But final thoughts and encouragement is not just about looking back, it's also about looking forward with optimism and excitement. For example, if you notice that things are not going as planned, you might need to remind yourself of your end goal and the reasons why you started your business in the first place. And with the right mindset and the right tools, you can overcome any obstacles and achieve success.

Congratulations on making it to the end of our guidebook! You should be proud of yourself for taking the initiative to start and grow your small business. Along the way, you've gained valuable insights and knowledge on market research, financial management, marketing strategies and operations, and so much more. Now, as you reach the final thoughts and encouragement section, it's time to reflect on your journey and celebrate your successes. You've come a long way, and you should be proud of the progress you've made. It's important to remember that starting and running a small business is not easy, but you've proven to yourself that you have what it takes to make it happen. This guidebook has been your personal guide and mentor, providing you with the encouragement and support to reach your desired financial outcomes. With the right mindset and the right tools, you've been able to navigate the marketplace and stand out from the competition. You've built a thriving brand and have the potential to take it even further. As you continue on your path to success, always remember to stay motivated, stay energized and keep pushing forward. You've got this!

www.ingramcontent.com/pod-product-compliance
Lightning Source LLC
Chambersburg PA
CBHW031510150726
47990CB00007B/2959